A Guide To Puglia

Five Walking Tours

P S Quick

ACORN BOOKS

Published in 2017 by
Acorn Books
www.acornbooks.co.uk

Acorn Books is an imprint of
Andrews UK Limited
www.andrewsuk.com

Contents

Introduction

Although not one of Italy's top tourist destinations Puglia is beginning to attract tourists to its varied charms. Once just the area where travellers arrived or departed for Greece, Albania and Croatia, Puglia is becoming appreciated for its own attractions. This area in the heel of Italy's boot has a rich historic past. Originally a humble farming region it has been influenced by Greeks, Romans, Normans and Byzantines who each made an impact on the landscape by building ports, churches and other magnificent buildings.

This book aims to give the tourist an opportunity to visit and enjoy not only the few major attractions that a guided tour usually includes but many of the other interesting sights that other people do not see. By providing five different walking routes and detailed information about each attraction passed it puts a visitor to Puglia in charge of the time spent at any particular place rather than having to rush and keep up with a guide or join costly tours.

These five walks will enable you to experience the variety and atmosphere of some wonderful contrasting destinations in Puglia. You will be surprised to discover the rich historical monuments of Brindisi and astounded by the Baroque architecture of Lecce; you'll marvel at the unique construction of the Trulli of Alberobello and be transported back in time when exploring the Sassi of Matera.

Preparation

- Puglia has a wonderful Mediterranean climate with short mild winters but the summers can be intensely hot and dry. Plan your trip according to the activities you wish to experience. If you visit in summer, particularly in July and August when temperatures can reach 30° and above, you will need to escape the sun for at least part of the day and may not see all you wish. April and May or September and October are good for sightseeing. The coldest month is January but it is still mild with an average of 10° while November is the wettest month.

- If you enjoy the pomp and ceremony of festivals then Puglia has a number throughout the year especially around Eastertime. Check online to confirm the festival's dates as they vary from year to year.

- Visit a tourist office as soon as you can on arrival to pick up details of attractions and opening times together with a free map which is essential in order to get your bearings and understand where places are located. Remember that Puglia is still developing as a tourist destination so there may be fewer resources available than in the more popular resorts of Italy. Hotels sometimes have free maps and other information for their clients.

- Do your research and read through this guide in order to decide which museums or other places you want to go into before leaving home. Puglia has some excellent museums that reflect its history and cultural heritage. Many are closed on Mondays so it is worth checking the opening times.

There will also be variations depending upon the time of year. In the south of Italy almost everything closes for lunch and does not reopen until late afternoon.

- Puglia has some wonderful places to take refreshment and try a range of local wines or food specialities such as burrata and pettola. While it is wonderful to sit and enjoy a drink or meal in the busy plazas next to top attractions this can be expensive. You will find some good quality tapas bars, cafes and restaurants off the main streets. Ask your hotel where the locals eat for the best deals.

- Transport links to the area are improving. It is possible to fly into Bari or Brindisi airport from where there are coaches and trains to many of the surrounding towns so hiring a car is not essential although can be useful for some of the smaller destinations.

- Public transport within some smaller towns is limited. You will see much more and absorb the atmosphere of the places in this guide if you can walk around the sites. However, some of the destinations such as Matera can be quite challenging if you have problems with walking. Most tours in this book are quite intense so you may want to spread some over two days. If you can, try to stay for a night in each of these destinations and enjoy the extra time. Spending a night in a Trulli in Alberobello or a Sassi cave in Matera will be an experience never forgotten.

- Prepare for your trip by trying to learn a few Italian words. Take a phrase book with you because in this area of Italy many people will not understand much English. Print out all your travel details and write a few things down in Italian so that you can show to people if you have any difficulties. The people are friendly and very willing to help.

The Tours

The First Tour: Brindisi

Known as the *Gateway to the East* since ancient times when it was an important port for Roman troops and later for Venetian merchants Brindisi has played a significant role in trade and culture. Today the city is a major port not only trading with the Middle East and Greece but also providing important travel connections by sea, air and train. There are good transport links to many of the other interesting towns in Puglia from Brindisi.

Many people view Brindisi merely as a location for arrivals and departures but Brindisi is a city worth exploring. It has a rich history that goes back to Greek and Roman times with two columns erected to pinpoint ancient Brindisi known as *Brundisium* as the end of the Appian Way. Since then it has passed to the Ostrogoths, the Byzantines, the Lombards, the Saracens and then the Normans. Brindisi became the port from where the Crusaders departed. Emperor Frederick II set off to the Sixth Crusade from this port and reclaimed Jerusalem for the Christians.

Brindisi was badly bombed during World War II and today's city is significantly different from the past. The seafront promenade is filled with restaurants and bars, the town centre has beautiful wide tree lined streets and yet the old part of the town still retains its winding streets filled with Baroque churches. The impressive fortress or *Castello Svevo* named after Emperor Frederick II now belongs to the Navy so cannot be visited. It has not been included in this tour but if you have time to spare then walk around the outside on another occasion.

Today's tour begins at the Piazza Santa Teresa then visits the tourist office in order to pick up a map before exploring the older parts of the town. It takes you through winding city streets where you will see architecture that spans centuries with churches, palaces, plazas, Roman columns and walls and the old city gates. The tour ends at Porta Lecce where you can also visit the Chiesa del Cristo.

Main Sights

- Piazza and Chiesa di Santa Teresa
- Monumento ai Caduti d'Italia
- Casa del Turista
- Colonne Romane
- Piazza Vittorio Emanuele II
- Piazza Della Vittoria
- Saint Pietro of Schiavoni Archeological Area
- Palazzo Granafei Nervegna
- Loggia del Palazzo Balsamo
- Cattedrale di San Giovanni Battista
- Seminario Arcivescovile
- Portico de Cavalieri Templari
- Museo Archeologico Provinciale "Francesco Ribezzo"
- San Giovanni Al Sepolcro
- Chiesa San Benedetto
- Porta Mesagne e Bastione Aragonese
- Piazza Cairoli
- Porta Lecce e Bastione di Levante
- Chiesa del Cristo

Piazza Santa Teresa

The large Square of Saint Teresa is located to the north of the old town and overlooks the seafront. From here there are steps leading down to the waterfront promenade. In the square you will find a monument to the fallen of World War I, the Church of Saint Teresa and a convent that now houses the state archives. The semi-circular Empire Fountain, also known as the Monumental Fountain, was built in 1940 and stands on the rounded outer part of the square.

Monumento ai Caduti d'Italia

In the centre of the square stands a striking memorial to the fallen Italians of World War I built from white Carrara marble by the local sculptor Edgardo Simone. The sculpture was originally intended for the railway station but has been moved a number of times as the sculptor thought the locations too trivial.

The figure at the top represents victory. In her right hand she holds a dagger with laurel and oak while in her left the city of Rome. A dying warrior holding a Roman shield carved with the head of Medusa lies at her feet. There are two figures that stand on either side. On the left is a mother sending her son off to war while on the right a mother has her arm around a young child and sits with her head bowed in grief. A record of all the major battles that Italy fought in World War I is engraved on the rear pedestal.

Chiesa Santa Teresa

On the eastern side of the square stands the Baroque Church of Saint Teresa with its adjoining cloisters which was built as a convent church in 1670 and dedicated to the Carmelites. The church has a splendid façade divided into three orders and decorated niches and two pinnacles connected by elegant spirals.

The Baroque Church of Saint Teresa

Inside the church has a single nave and transept with small chapels. It holds some valuable paintings. On the high altar are two paintings by Diego Bianchi, *San Giuseppe* and *Ecstasy of Saint Teresa*. There are the outstanding canvases of *Saint Andrew* and *Our Lady of Mount Carmel* and a number of statues including the stone statue of *Saint Francis of Paola*. In the chapel dedicated to the Medici saints there are five papier-mâché statues.

The suppressed convent next to the church which was dedicated to Saint Joachim and Saint Andrew was used as a military headquarters in 1807 but now holds the state records. Look to the side of the church along the narrow street Via Moricino to see the *Case-Mediterranean* dwellings built for the less wealthy inhabitants of the city.

Walk south-east on Piazza Santa Teresa. Turn left onto Via Annibale de Leo, left after 80 metres onto Via Montenegro then right again after 140 metres onto Viale Regina Margherita. The tourist office will be on the right after 80 metres.

Casa del Turista

The ancient and important building now known as the Tourist House dates back to the times of the Crusaders and was originally owned by the Knights Templar although it has since been modified. On the outside you can still see the arc of entrance on the keystone and the Maltese cross which was the symbol of the Templars.

From here you can look across the Pigonati Channel and see the Sailor's Monument across the bay which was built in 1933 in the shape of a rudder. It stands fifty-four metres tall and is crowned with a statue of Our Lady. If you have longer than a day in Brindisi it is worth visiting. Inside there is a beautiful oval staircase and a fantastic panoramic view from the top of the tower.

At the base of the column is a sacred chapel built in memory of the fallen soldiers from both World Wars and there is the bell from the battleship *Benedetto Brin* which sank in the harbour in 1915 as well as two anchors from other battleships.

Walk south-east on Viale Regina Margherita for 160 metres then turn right and take the stairs. The Colonne Romane will be on the right after 40 metres.

Colonne Romane

Once two Roman columns stood in this square and were thought to symbolise the end of the Appian Way for navigators. The columns were seen as a symbol of Brindisi but today only one remains intact although you can still see the base of the other column which fell down in 1528. The remainder of this column was given to the city of Lecce to form part of the Saint Oronzo column.

The original capital of the remaining column can be seen in the museum of the Palazzo Granafei Nervegna as the one in the square is a copy. It is decorated with an anthropomorphic design on each of its sides. Neptune faces the sea while Jupiter, Mars and Minerva can be seen on the other sides.

On the right of the square are the remains of the house in which the Latin poet Virgil died. The archaeological museum of Faldetta, also known as *Palazzina del Belvedere,* the Belvedere

The Virgil Steps leading up to the Roman Columns

Palace, can be found in this square. It has a collection of over three hundred and fifty artefacts and offers a good view of the harbour from its rooftop. The stairs that lead up to the square are known as the *Virgil Steps*.

Take the stairs then turn right onto Viale Regina Margherita. After 200 metres turn right onto Piazza Vittorio Emanuele II and continue until you reach Piazza Vittorio Emanuele II.

Piazza Vittorio Emanuele II

The Vittorio Emanuele Square and its gardens were renovated in 2001. Here you will find the Dolphin's Fountain which was built in 1876 by Belliazzi. The marble Virgil's Monument from 1988 is the work of Floriano Bodini and also the Gothic Dionisi building. On the harbour office wall there is a sundial built in 1917 by Captain Alberto de Albertis.

To the left of the Lungomare Regina Margherita are two more plaques on the harbour-office building. The first is a marble epigraph in memory of the Serbian refugees who were rescued during the war. The other is a bronze plate known as the *Honourable War Merit Cross* which was awarded for Brindisi's war effort.

Walk south-west on Piazza Vittorio Emanuele II for 30 metres. Turn left to stay on this road. After 60 metres turn right onto Corso Giuseppe Garibaldi then walk for 300 metres before turning right onto Piazza Della Vittoria.

Piazza Della Vittoria

Victory Square is one of the main squares in Brindisi and is home to many shops and bars. It has been created from two former squares, one known as the *Square of the Nobles* and the other the *Square of the People*. Once a market square it is famous for the historic fountain that was built in 1618 by the royal governor Peter Louis de Torres.

Known as the *Fontana de Torres* the fountain stands in the middle of the square. It was one of the first to bring drinking water from the aqueduct to Brindisi's citizens, the soldiers of the Spanish galleon which was anchored in the harbour and the market users. All citizens contributed financially to the construction of the fountain. A marble basin that had previously served as a christening font in medieval times was used and four spouts were attached to it.

Walk north-west on the Piazza, turn right onto Via Raffaele Rubini for 15 metres, left at Via Filimeno Consiglio for 17 metres then right onto Via Santi. After 130 metres the Saint Pietro of Schiavoni Archeologica Area will be on the right.

Saint Pietro of Schiavoni Archeological Area

The archaeological area of Saint Peter of Schiavoni is located below the Verdi New Theatre in the heart of ancient Brindisi and is accessible from Piazzetta Giustino Durano. The Schiavoni were mainly Greek and Albanian people who lived in the area. There is no longer any trace of the church that stood here and gave the area its name.

When a number of dilapidated houses were demolished in the early sixties to build a new courthouse and theatre the remains of a medieval city were discovered. Building works were halted as important relics of the medieval city were being destroyed. Eventually a Roman *insula* was discovered. Original building plans were changed and it was decided to construct a huge suspended steel theatre over the area so it remained accessible to everyone.

The area is crossed in a north to south direction by a paved road located in several private and public buildings and is important as it shows what the road network of the early Roman city was like. On the sides of the road there are sidewalks and it is possible to see the grooves made by wagons in places. Here too are the remains of the early dwellings paved with earthenware tiles laid in a herringbone pattern. In the south-western part there are a number of rooms paved with mosaics, terracotta and earthenware pesto. A spa complex was found in the south-eastern sector.

In the northern area nineteen burials dating to the Middle Ages were found, linked to a church with a marble floor. The church appears to have been built over a Roman *Domus* that had white marble tiles bordered by black tiles with a central multi-coloured emblem, a marble griffin and other sculptures.

Many artefacts were found during the phases of excavation such as an old Christian sarcophagus, marble sculptures, statuettes, ornaments and pottery. These can be seen in the Provincial Museum Ribezzo.

Walk north for 36 metres and turn right onto Via del Balzo. Turn right after 35 metres onto Via Duomo. The Palazzo Granafei Nervegna will be on the left after 35 metres.

Palazzo Granafei Nervegna

The Palace of the Granafei and Nervegna families is an historic Brindisi mansion built in 1565 for Donato Ferrante. It was then owned by Nicholas Granafei who came from Constantinople and rose to become Mayor of the city. It passed to the Nervenga family in the eighteenth century.

The building is of Renaissance style but with some Baroque features such as the railings of the balconies. The main façade is divided into three levels by string courses that have four Latin inscriptions. The building has many windows and decorations. The portal is surmounted by the coat of arms of the Granafei family which depicts a rampant lion carrying an ear of corn. It is thought that Nicholas was a grain trader in Constantinople hence the name *grana fert*. Today it is possible to visit the interior of the building to see a number of artefacts including the original Roman capital.

Walk north on Via Duomo for 110 metres. The Loggia Balsamo will be signposted on the left.

Loggia del Palazzo Balsamo

Opposite the Seminary building you can see the fourteenth century Balsamo Palace that was probably part of a much larger block of buildings. It is thought that the Angevin mint was located here. The oldest and most interesting part of the building is the Loggia or lodge which is a balcony supported by brackets placed on two pointed arches. It has eight fine arches that contain sculptured allegorical figures of people and animals.

Walk north-east on Via Giovanni Tarantini keeping right to stay on this road until you reach Piazza Duomo.

Piazza Duomo

The beautiful Cathedral Square is the oldest square in the city. Here, having just passed the Loggia of the Balsamo Palace, you will find the Cathedral, the Seminary, the Knights Templar Portico and the Provincial Archaeological Museum. The square which was originally known as the *Bishop's Square* was once the Roman town centre. Between the Cathedral and the Roman columns there stood the spectacular temple of Apollo and Diana. Stones from this temple have been used to build the Cathedral.

The Knights Templar, Ribezzo Museum and Cathedral in Cathedral Square

Cattedrale della Visitazione e di San Giovanni Battista

The Cathedral dedicated to the Visitation and Saint John the Baptist was consecrated in 1089 by Pope Urban II and completed in 1143. It was here that Ruggiero, the son of Tancredi, was crowned King of Sicily in 1191 and later married Irene. In 1225 Emperor Frederico II married Isabella of Brienne. Since then the cathedral has been almost entirely rebuilt after the earthquake in 1743 although parts of the original mosaic floor can still be seen inside.

The main façade has undergone a number of changes even in very recent years. The statues of Saint Theodore, Saint Lawrence, Saint Leucio of Alexandria and Pope Pius X that replaced the tympanum in 1957 were replaced again during the renovation of 2007. Sculptured from local stone they represent Saint Justine of Jacobis, Saint Theodore of Amasea, Saint Leucio and Saint Lawrence of Brindisi.

The Romanesque building has a Baroque bell tower that was built in 1780. The Cathedral is built on a Latin cross design with a nave and two aisles but there is no transept. The relics of Saint Theodor, the patron saint of Brindisi, can be found in the chapel. There is a stunning sixteenth century wooden choir and a baptismal font decorated with four stone cherubs also dating from the sixteenth century.

The Cathedral holds many valuable paintings and frescos such as the *Last Supper* by Diego O White and the *Judgement of Solomon*. The ornate dome has four paintings relating to Moses. These are *Moses and the Serpent*, *Moses and the Sacrifice to God*, *Moses and the rock waters*, and *Moses and Manna from Heaven*. Many of the Baroque decorations have now been removed.

Seminario Arcivescovile

The Seminary building, also known as the Bishop's Palace, is the best example of Baroque architecture in Brindisi. Designed by Mauro Maniere from Lecce it was built from white marble and completed in 1720. On the main façade are eight ornamental statues that are allegories to the highest branches of knowledge and depict Philosophy, Theology, Ethics, Mathematics, Eloquence, Law, Poetics and Harmony.

Inside there is a splendid chapel, a library with over one hundred and twenty thousand books and the Diocesan Museum which holds a number of archaeological artefacts and sacred art. Particularly worth viewing is the *Idria delle Nozze di Cana* which is said to be one of the six vases in which Jesus performed his first miracle turning water into wine. It is the only vase to have survived. The museum also holds the silver ark containing the remains of Saint Theodore and a parchment paper signed by Emperor Federico II.

Portico de Cavalieri Templari

The Portico of the Knights Templar is a medieval building thought to date back to the twelfth century. A Greek marble pillar with a decorated capital separates the two Gothic arches built from Carparo limestone.

Museo Archeologico Provinciale "Francesco Ribezzo"

The Provincial Archaeological Museum named after the archaeologist and linguist Francesco Ribezzo is also located in Cathedral Square. It has a number of large rooms in which you can view epigraphic inscriptions, Roman statues found in Brindisi, an ancient section with Apulian vases and coins, a prehistoric section, a collection of coins from different eras and the famous *Punta del Serrone Bronzes*.

Walk south on Via Santa Chiara for 35 metres turning right to stay on the road. Turn left after 23 metres onto Via Giovanni Tarantini. Walk for 190 metres, turn left onto Via Marco Pacuvio for 70 metres, turn right onto Via San Giovanni al Sepolcro and the Chiesa San Giovanni al Sepolcro will be on the left after 40 metres.

San Giovanni Al Sepolcro

The Temple of Saint John of the Tomb is a circular building constructed at the end of the eleventh century. Used by the Knights Templar it is one of the finest examples of Romanesque architecture in Southern Italy and is thought to have been inspired by the Holy Sepulchre in Jerusalem. The circular base has walls made from carparo limestone.

The Temple of Saint John of the Tomb

The main portal is framed with a marble architrave, two columns standing upon marble lions and capitals with fantastic figures. The sides of the door are richly decorated with scenes from battles between real and mythological animals. Inside there are eight columns topped with capitals decorated with acanthus leaves. A wooden roof has replaced the original vaulted one. The wall frescos depict saints dating from the twelfth to fifteenth centuries.

The temple was used as a museum between 1850 and 1955 and became a centre for cultural meetings attended by renowned figures such as Mahatma Gandhi and the Indian poet Rabindranath Tagore.

Walk north-west on Via San Giovanni al Sepolcro for 60 metres then turn left onto Via Piertommaso Santabarbara, left after110 metres onto Via San Benedetto then right after 95 metres onto Via Guglielmo Marconi. The Chiesa San Benedetto will be on the right after 40 metres.

Chiesa San Benedetto

The Church of Saint Benedict is another typical example of Romanesque art and was built in 1809 with an adjoining convent dedicated to the Benedictine nuns. The original church was completely different from the present one. The façade has a series of blind arches with small lancet windows and a portal with architrave depicting hunting scenes between men and dragons. The belfry is lit by blind arches and three mullioned windows.

Inside the recently restored church has three naves and four bays created by arches resting on columns. Four of the marble columns are Corinthian and have superb Romanesque capitals. The mediaeval cloister of the former monastery can be accessed from within the church.

Walk south-west on Via Guglielmo Marconi for 120 metres. Turn left onto Via San Margherita then right after 110 metres onto Via Carmine. The Porta Mesagne e Bastione Aragonese will be on the left after 75 metres.

Porta Mesagne e Bastione Aragonese

The Mesagne Gate is the oldest entrance to the city. The arched entrance is of Swebian design dating back to around 1243 but its foundations stand on the original Roman ramparts. There is also a smaller arched entrance that was built in the 1930's.

If you pass through the gate and turn right you will find the ruins of the Roman aqueducts known as *Vasche Limarie* that collected drinking water from the *Pozzo de Vito*, which is 12 kilometres away. The water flowed through several tanks containing sand in order to cleanse it before being distributed to the fountains of Brindisi.

Walk east on Via Carmine for 20 metres then turn right onto Via Cristoforo Colombo. After 40 metres turn left onto Via Leopardi, right after 85 metres onto Via Giordano Bruno and left after 170 metres onto Corso Umberto I. The Piazza Cairoli will be ahead after 60 metres.

Piazza Cairoli

The Piazza Cairoli is a large square surrounded by shops, cafes and restaurants where you can take refreshment towards the end of this tour. There are a number of seats within the square where you can relax and watch the world go by. It is a beautiful square to visit at night when the fountain is lit.

The square is famous for the *Fontana delle Ancore*, the Fountain of the Anchors, which dates back to 1937. The original fountain had just one central jet but ten years later two large frogs and turtles were added so it became known as the *Fountain of the Frogs*. In 1937 these were removed and the present fountain was erected. The fountain has a large central jet with four big stone anchors representing the symbol of a compass.

Walk east and take the Via Alfrredo Cappellini exit from the roundabout. Continue for 130 metres onto Via Giovanni XXIII for 140 metres then turn right onto Via Giuseppe da Roma. The Porta Lecce e Bastione di Levante will be on the right after 48 metres.

Porta Lecce e Bastione di Levante

The Porta Lecce is an ancient city gate built in 1464 on the orders of Ferdinand of Aragon and later enhanced by Charles V in 1530. Look above the arch and you will see the coat of Arms of Charles in the centre, Ferdinando Alarcon on the left and the city of Brindisi on the right.

The gate was protected with the Aragon walls on either side dating back to the fifteenth century with ramparts and strategically placed towers. Within the tunnel formed by the gate were places where the military and defence needs could be addressed. Today these are used for exhibitions and special events. It is possible to walk along the walls and also climb the steps to walk along the top where you can enjoy the views. While you are here take the opportunity to visit the Chiesa del Cristo that can be accessed from the square.

Chiesa del Cristo

The Church of the Crucifix was built upon the request of Brother Nicholas Paglia of Giovinazzo for the Dominicans in 1232 with an adjacent convent. The church has a striking façade created by alternating courses of grey and red stones with a magnificent rose window over the main door. The window has two concentric bands decorated with plant motifs and a halo of sixteen columns. Above these is another half band supported by two columns. To the sides of the window are a number of blind arches.

Above the carved wooden portal is a relief of the Crucifix with Saint Nicholas Paglia and Saint Dominic of Guzman to the sides. Look to the left of the portal in the lighter band of stone to see the foundation date of the church.

Inside the church has a single nave with two Baroque side altars dedicated to Our Lady of the Rosary and the Sacred Heart. It has a trussed wooded roof and arched lancet. The church holds some valuable wooden sculptures such as *Our Lady of Light* by Lux Mundi and the wooded crucifix on the high altar.

The Second Tour: Lecce

The historic city of Lecce is one of the larger cities in Puglia and a magnet for tourists. It is sometimes described as *the Florence of the South* due to its numerous Baroque architecture and monuments. The city has links with the Greeks and Romans. It is still possible to view the Roman theatre and amphitheatre. Many of the magnificent palaces and churches with their intricate ornate facades were built in the seventeenth century using the local soft limestone in a style referred to as Lecce Baroque.

Transport links to Lecce are good. Brindisi airport is about forty-five kilometres away while the distance from Bari is around is one hundred and sixty kilometres. Lecce is on the main rail network and is connected to many other Italian towns. It takes around thirty minutes to reach Lecce from Brindisi and two hours from Bari by train. There is a direct coach link from the airport to Lecce. The train and coach stations are about a kilometre from the city centre. Taking the bus into town is a cheaper option than a taxi.

To explore Lecce to its full you need at least a full day but preferably two. There are various tourist offices and information kiosks around the city such as in Piazza Sant'Oronzo, next to the Cathedral and the castle. Pick up a map of Lecce to get your bearings as soon as you can.

There are a number of hotels and also many places offering bed and breakfast. Lecce has a selection of restaurants around the historic centre and in the streets beyond. Don't miss the chance to visit the popular *Gelateria Pasticceria Natale* which is said to be Lecce's finest cake and ice cream shop.

Today's tour begins in the Piazzetta Arco di Trionfo at Porta Napoli which is one of the main city gates. It takes you through the historic area of the town and other parts too providing opportunities to appreciate the magnificent architecture as you pass palaces, museums, churches, the two other city gates, famous monuments, picturesque plazas and beautiful gardens.

Main Sights

- Piazzetta Arco di Trionfo
- Porta Napoli and Obelisco
- Palazzo Guarini
- Chiesa Santa Maria della Porta
- Chiesa Delle Alcantarine
- Chiesa di Sant'Angelo
- Palazzo Taurino
- Basilica di Santa Croce
- Palazzo dei Celestini
- Castello Carlo V and Fontana Dell'Armonia
- Chiesa di Santa Maria della Grazia
- Piazza Sant'Oronzo and Colonna Sant'Oronzo
- Anfiteatro Romano
- Chiesa San Marco y Palacio Sedile
- Chiesa di Santa Chiara
- Porta San Biagio
- Museo Faggiano
- Parrocchia San Matteo
- Palazzo Carrozzo
- Museo y Teatro Romano
- Duomo di Lecce and Torre Campanaria
- Palazzo Arcivescovile and Seminario Palazzo
- Basilica di San Giovanni Battista del Rosario
- Porta Rudiae

Baroque decoration on the Church of Saint John the Baptist

Piazzetta Arco di Trionfo

The Arch of Triumph Square is a beautiful plaza lined with trees that links the Porta Napoli Obelisk and the Porta Napoli Gate.

Obelisco di Porta Napoli

The Porta Napoli obelisk was designed by Luigi Cepolla and built by the sculptor Vito Carluccio. It was erected in 1822 to commemorate the visit of King Ferdinand I of Bourbon. The square obelisk is about ten metres in height and stands on a pedestal that has a dolphin biting a crescent on each side representing the coat of arms of Terra d'Otranto.

The four sides of the obelisk are decorated with mythological badges and the coats of arms of Brindisi, Gallipoli, Lecce and Taranto. Look out for the cockerel, scorpion, deer and wolf.

From the Obelisk walk south-east along the Piazza Arco di Triunfo. The Porta Napoli will be ahead.

Porta Napoli

The Gate of Naples, also known as the Arch of Triumph, was erected in 1548 on the site of the ancient Porta San Giusto, to honour Charles V for having fortified the town by rebuilding the castle and erecting the city walls. The triumphal arch is twenty metres tall and has a triangular pediment supported on each side by two columns with Corinthian capitals. In the centre is the coat of arms of Charles V. Under the pediment is an inscription praising King Charles for his accomplishments.

Under the road near this area excavations have revealed parts of the Messapian walls of the city, dating from the late fourth century BC.

Pass through the Porta Napoli and turn right to view the Palazzo Guarini and the Chiesa Santa Maria della Porta.

Palazzo Guarini

The beautiful Guarini palace was originally built in the sixteenth century but renovated in the eighteenth century by the architect Mauro Manieri. The façade was designed using the Rocco style and has a number of balconies with superb cornices and a magnificent portal.

The hall inside has arches and a balustrade while the stunning courtyard is accessed through a gateway with an arched lintel. In the garden an underground tomb was discovered that dates to around 350 BC. The palace is famous for the visits of Giuseppe Bonaparte in 1807 and Gioacchino Murat in 1813.

Chiesa Santa Maria della Porta

The Church of Saint Mary of the Gate was originally a small chapel outside the city walls with a statue of the Virgin that can be seen within the present church. When the walls were rebuilt in the sixteenth century it was expanded and built within the walls. The current building was designed by the architect Joseph Maiola of Maddaloni in a Neo-Classical style in the nineteenth century.

The main façade has a doorway with Doric columns and a triangular pediment above. The church has a central octagonal design with arches that support the dome. There are two aisles and the church is lit by the skylight at the top of the dome and six semi-circular windows while the beautiful altar encloses the golden tabernacle. Above the altar in the central chapel is a sculpture of the Madonna della Porta.

Walk south on Via Giuseppe Palmieri for 15 metres passing the Teatro Paisiello on the left. Turn left onto Via Leonardo Prato. Walk for 200 metres then turn right onto Piazzetta Arco Di Prato.

Piazzetta Arco Di Prato

The Arch of Prato was named by Brother Leonardo Prato who was a captain of the Order of the Knights of Jerusalem in the fifteenth century. The arch is supported by enormous square pillars, above which is a loggia with columns and fluted pilasters. Look out for the coat of arms of the Prato family.

Walk north on Piazzetta Arco di Prato. Turn right onto Via Leonardo Prato, left after 45 metres onto Via Francesco AntonioD'Amelio, left after 110 metres onto Via Idomeneo, right after 75 metres onto Via Conte Gaufrido then left after 70 metres onto Vicolo Protonobilissimi. The Chiesa Delle Alcantarine will be on the right after 12 metres.

Chiesa Delle Alcantarine

The Church of the Alcantarine, also known as the Church of Saint Mary of Providence, was built in the early eighteenth century by the architect Giuseepe Cino and later modified by Mauro Manieri. The attractive façade is formed by three superimposed orders with decorative elements. The lower level has alternating pilasters with niches in between that have the statues of Saint Raphael the Archangel, Saint Anthony of Padua, Saint Francis of Assisi and Saint Michael the Archangel.

On the second level there is a central window framed with small pillars and two niches with statures of Saint Peter of Alcantara on the left and Saint Paschal Baylon to right. Above the window on the top level is a curved tympanum with gables and swirls on small square pillars.

Inside the rectangular nave has three chapels on each side and a vaulted roof decorated with light stucco while the nineteenth century floor is paved with polychrome glazed bricks. Look out for the seventeen century canvas of the *Adoration of the Shepherds* by Diego Bianchi and the eighteenth century paintings of the *Virgin and Child* and the *Crucifixion.*

Walk south-east on Vicolo Protonobilissimi for 12 metres. Turn left onto Piazzetta Baglivi Giorgio, left again after 70 metres to stay on this road then right after 8 metres onto Vico San Giusto. The Chiesa di Sant'Angelo will be on the left after 35 metres.

Chiesa di Sant'Angelo

The Church of Saint Angelo was one of the first churches to be built in Lecce. Built around 1061 by the Augustinians it was originally outside the city walls. The church was rebuilt in the fourteenth century and in 1661 completely redesigned by Giuseppe Zimbalo in its present opulent Baroque style.

The façade has a beautiful portal set between two columns and a bronze door dating from 1750 designed by Emanuele Manieri. The lower part is divided by double pilasters and two columns in the centre with grooved drums decorated with cherubs and other ornaments. A statue of the Madonna and Child flanked by two angels stands in the curved pediment above the door.

The church is built on a Latin cross design and there are four chapels to each side with richly decorated Baroque altars. The church has a number of seventeenth century paintings worth viewing as well as the eighteenth century *Judgement of Solomon* and *Solomon and Sheba.*

The Church of Saint Angelo

Walk north-east on Vico San Giusto. After 20 metres turn right onto Piazza Addolorata, left after 70 metres onto Vicolo Renzi then right after 5 metres onto Via Manfredi. Turn left after 75 metres onto Via Umberto I then right after 10 metres to stay on this road. Visit the Plazzo dei Celestini last as you can walk through the courtyard to the public gardens then continue this tour.

Palazzo Taurino

This Jewish museum housed in the Taurino Palace provides a fascinating insight into the Jewish life of Lecce during the Middle Ages. It holds a number of Jewish artefacts and also offers the opportunity to watch a short film. The museum is in the old *giudecca*, on the site of the ancient synagogue.

Basilica di Santa Croce

The construction of the Baroque church of the Holy Cross was begun in 1353 but not completed until 1695. The magnificent façade of the church is richly decorated with six columns supporting a cornice embellished with animals, vegetables and grotesque figures. There are four small rose windows on the lower level and a large central rose window above the balustrade on the upper level over the door. On either side of the large rose window are two Corinthian columns which separate the central area from the sides where there are niches containing the statues of Saint Benedict and Pope Celestine V. At the sides stand two large female statues symbolising Faith and Fortitude.

The main portal is flanked by pairs of Corinthian columns. Look out for the coats of arms of Philip III of Spain, Mary of Enghien and Walter VI of Brienne and those of the Celestines on the side portals. There are several statues representing the Turkish prisoners taken during the Battle of Lepanto in 1571. Under the balustrade are animals symbolising the people who took part in the battle such as Hercules, the griffon and a dragon.

The church is built on a Latin cross design and originally had a nave with a rich wooden ceiling and four aisles although two were turned into side chapels in the eighteenth century. The church has seventeen altars with the main altar displaying the coat of arms of the Adorni family whose tombs can be seen inside the church. There are paintings of a *Trinity* by Gianserio Strafella, the *Adoration of the Shepherd* by Giovanni Battista Lama and *Saint Antony of Padua* by Oronzo Tiso.

Palazzo dei Celestini

The stunning Baroque Celestini Palace is next to the Chiesa di Santa Croce and was the convent of the Celestine fathers for three hundred years, established in 1352. Today it is home to the Government Hall of Lecce.

The present complex was designed by Riccardi and built in 1549. The façade has columns and decorations that frame the twenty windows. The two on the upper level have balustrades. The central portal is decorated with fruit branches and angels while the atrium is framed by forty-four columns with twenty-four arches. It is possible to walk through the courtyard of the building to reach the public gardens.

Walk through the Palazzo dei Celestini to join Via XXV Luglio then turn right. The Public Gardens will be on the left. It is also possible to reach this road after visiting the Palazzo Taurino by turning left onto Via Archille Costa which brings you out at the corner of the gardens.

Giardini Pubblici

The Public Gardens are well worth a visit for their interest and tranquillity. The main entrance can be accessed from Via XXV Luglio. The project for the gardens was drafted in 1818. They were constructed in 1830 under the direction of Gaetano Stella but in 1883 the gardens came under new management and were named the Giuseppe Garibaldi gardens.

The gardens are designed upon a formal Italian style with symmetrical walkways that traverse the park. There are plenty of seats where you can relax, admire the varieties of trees and flowers or simply watch the world go by. In the centre is a beautiful domed pavilion while the rest of the park has numerous decorative and architectural elements such as fountains and ponds. As you wander around you will see the stone and marble busts of twenty-two famous people, the first of which was built in 1874. They are signed by different artists such as Eugene Maccagnani and Giuseppe Mangionello.

Continue south on Via Umberto for 240 metres. The Castello Carlo V will be on the left.

Castello Carlo V

Originally built in the twelfth century the Castle of Charles V was reconstructed in the sixteenth century together with the city walls on the orders of Charles V who wanted to fortify the town. Designed by the architect Gian Giacomo the castle is the largest in Puglia.

Visitors to the castle can enjoy the architecture and the decorative internal ornamentation. As well as the majestic stairs, the imposing stone columns on the upper floors and the impressive stained glass windows there is an internal portal dating back to 1500 which leads into the great hall of the main building with its finely carved capitals.

There are a number of displays about the history of the castle. The castle is now home to Lecce's department of Cultural Affairs and exhibitions of art are held within the rooms.

Continue walking south on Via XXV for 95 metres then turn right onto Via Vito Fazzi. Walk west for 80 metres then turn right onto Via Alvino. The Chiesa di Santa Maria della Grazia will be on the right.

Chiesa di Santa Maria della Grazia

The beautiful Baroque Church of Saint Mary of Grace was designed by Michele Coluccio and built between 1590 and 1606 on the site of an old chapel. The elegant façade is divided into two levels. The lower has pilasters and fluted columns enclosing an ornate portal with statues of Saint Peter and Saint Paul in the niches to the sides.

The triangular pediment is embellished with a carving of the Madonna and Child with five angels above them. The upper level has a large window and two empty niches.

The interior of the church is built on a Latin cross design with a single nave and a beautiful walnut coffered ceiling by Allipoli Vespasiano Genuino. There is a fourteenth century fresco of the *Virgin and Child* and paintings by Oronzo Tiso depicting the *Assumption*, the *Adoration of the Shepherds and the Archangel Michael* and the wooden crucifix by Vespasiano Genuino.

Continue along Via Alvino. You will see the Roman amphitheatre and the Piazza Sant'Oronzo beyond.

Piazza Sant'Oronzo

Piazza Saint Oronzo is the main square in Lecce, named after the Roman Column and statue of Saint Oronzo that stands there. It was originally known as *Piazza dei Mercanti*, the merchants' square, where all the shops and commerce were located. It was the location for religious processions, military battles, scenes of torture and riots.

The square has a wealth of monuments and until the last century no-one knew about the Roman amphitheatre that lay beneath their feet. It was only discovered when excavations were made for the construction of the Bank of Italy in 1901.

The layout of the square was changed to reveal as much of the amphitheatre as possible. The Roman column that stood in the square was relocated to its present position. Look out for the two ancient olive trees in the square. In the centre of the square there is a mosaic depicting a wolf.

Anfiteatro Romano

Some parts of the Roman amphitheatre are still hidden beneath the street's historic buildings such as the Church of Santa Maria della Grazia. The amphitheatre was built in the second century. During the excavations when building in 1901 many architectural and sculptural elements of the building were discovered including some bas-reliefs portraying animal hunts.

*Piazza Sant'Oronzo with the Amphitheatre,
Sedile Palace and Oronzo Column*

Colonna Sant'Oronzo

Standing twenty-nine metres high the Roman column with the statue of Saint Oronzo on top dominates the square.

In Brindisi there were once two Roman columns that marked the end of the Appian Way. When one of them crumbled the pieces were donated to Lecce. Between 1666 and 1681 the column was rebuilt in Lecce with a statue of Saint Oronzo on the top. Lecce had miraculously escaped the plague that raged through southern Italy and this was attributed to the saint.

The original copper coated wooden statue was burned during a celebration in 1737 so a new bronze effigy was cast in Venice and placed on the column in 1739. To ensure its preservation the statue was removed during the Second World War and kept in the cathedral then replaced once the war had ended.

Chiesa San Marco y Palacio Sedile

The Church of Saint Mark stands next to the Seat Palace. Saint Mark's Church was designed by the architect Gabriele Riccardi then built in 1543 for the thriving colony of Venetians who were living in the city.

The church comprises a single cubic block with a late Renaissance style façade. There is ornamentation around the rose window and also around the portal. Look out for the winged lion holding a book which is the symbol of Saint Mark.

The Seat Palace is a magnificent Gothic-Renaissance building dating to the late sixteenth century. The palace is cuboid in shape and has large pointed arches on the lower level and three rounded arches on each side on the upper level. It is beautifully decorated with regalia and coats of arms. Originally the place where governors held their public meetings today it hosts art shows and exhibitions.

From Piazza Sant'Oronzo walk west then turn right onto Via Augusto Imperatore. Walk for 140 metres then turn right onto Via Arte della Cartapesta and the Chiesa di Santa Chiara will be on the right.

Chiesa di Santa Chiara

The Church of Saint Clare is one of the most famous churches in Lecce. It was built in 1429 then modified in 1687. The lower part of the façade has fluted pilasters and columns with empty niches between although these are decorated with medallions and cartouches. Plant motifs decorate the portal which is topped with smiling angels and the emblem of the Clare nuns. On the higher level on either side of the large central window there are more niches flanked with fluted pilasters and a winged cherub.

Inside the church is beautiful with richly adorned altars and twisted columns. There are a number of wooden statues and paintings worth viewing including the canvas by Francesco Solimenta of *Saint Agnes* in the sacristy.

Walk east on Via Arte della Cartapesta for 10 metres. Continue onto Via Ludovico Maremonti bearing left after 190 metres to stay on this road then right after 90 metres onto Via Guglielmo Marconi. Continue for 70 metres. The Fontana Dell'Armonia will be on the left.

Fontana Dell'Armonia

The Fountain of Harmony was sculptured by Antonio Mazzotta from Trani stone and bronze to celebrate the water that was brought to the city from the Rive Sele through the Apulian aqueduct in 1927. The fountain is formed from pipes of various lengths that are bonded together. The water flows from the pipes into a circular basin below. The bronze statues that stand on the top are an allegory of youth and love.

Continue east on Via Guglielmo Marconi for 15 metres then turn right onto Viale Francesco Lo Re. After 280 metres turn right onto Piazza D'Italia. You will see the Porta San Biagio ahead.

Porta San Biagio

San Biagio is one of the three ancient gates of Lecce. It is dedicated to San Biagio who was Bishop of Sebaste in the fourth century. This southern gate to the city was rebuilt in 1771 on the order of the governor Tommaso Ruffo. It is a simple sombre gateway that stands just over seventeen metres tall with pairs of smooth columns resting on tall pedestals. Above the arch is the crest of Ferdinand IV of Bourbon and the coats of arms of Lecce. At the very top stands the statue of Saint Blaise in full episcopal robes.

Walk north-west for 12 metres to continue onto Via dei Perroni. Turn right onto Via Ascanio Grandi after 50 metres. The Museo Faggiano will be on the right.

Museo Faggiano

The Museum of the Faggiano family opened in 2008. The owner of the building had removed parts of the floor in order to replace some pipes. This led to the discovery of numerous objects and several ancient buildings. Beneath the ground was the floor of a *Messapi* house dating to the fifth century BC as well as Roman crypts, a Roman granary and medieval walls. There was also evidence that it was a Templar home and a convent for Franciscan nuns. This private museum is well worth a visit.

Walk south-west on Via Ascanio Grandi for 2 metres then turn right onto Via dei Perroni. After 80 metres the Parrocchia San Matteo will be on the right.

Parrocchia San Matteo

The Baroque Church of Saint Matthew was designed by Achille Larducci who was said to have been influenced by a church in Rome. It was built in 1667 on the site of a fifteenth century chapel. It is also known by locals as Santa Maria della Luce. The church has an interesting contrast of levels with the lower being convex and the higher concave.

Two columns on high bases divide the lower level. Look carefully and you will see one is decorated while the other is not. The door is elaborately embellished and has the crest of the Franciscan order above. On either side there are two niches. The top level has three mullioned windows in the centre with decorations of flowers and pine cones.

The large elliptical nave is divided by pilasters on which statues of the Apostles stand. There are small chapels along the side walls. As well as stone carvings and a wooden Pietà the church holds a number of interesting paintings.

Walk north-west on Via Federico D'Aragona for 13 metres then turn left onto Via Del Palazzo dei Conti di Lecce. The Palazzo Carrozzo will be on the left after 120 metres.

Palazzo Carrozzo

Located on the site of a sixteenth century monastery the Carrozzo Palace was once an elegant building designed by Emanuele Manieri and built in 1760. It has a concave façade with richly adorned doors, windows and balconies.

Walk west on Via del Palazzo dei Conti di Lecce for 50 metres, turn right onto Via Guglielmo Paladini for 95 metres then turn right onto Via degli Ammirati. The Museo del Teatro Romano will be on the right after 50 metres.

Museo y Teatro Romano

The museum was established by the Fondazione Memmo in the seventeenth century Roman palace. It holds a number of artefacts found when excavating the Roman Theatre in 1920 as well as reproductions of Roman monuments and an exhibition.

The Roman theatre dates from the second century and is the only example of civil architecture designed for a theatre in Puglia. Divided into six sections of steps where the audience sat by five radial stairways it is also possible to see the orchestra floor and stage. The original statues from the site are now housed in the Provincial Museum.

Walk back west on Via degli Ammirati for 50 metres then turn right onto Via Arcivescovo Petronelli. After 80 metres turn left onto Via Vittorio Emanuele II for 45 metres then left again onto Piazza del Duomo.

Piazza del Duomo

The religious centre of Lecce can be found in the historic Cathedral Square with its ornately decorated Baroque buildings. These include the Cathedral, the bell tower, the Bishop's Palace and the Seminary. The square is completely enclosed on three sides. In the past it was used as a courtyard during the day but closed in the evenings. Look carefully at the entrance to the square for the large stumps of the original gates.

Duomo di Lecce

The Cathedral of Our Lady of Assumption was originally built in 1144 then rebuilt in 1659 by the architect Guiseppe Zimbalo. The main portal on the northern façade is regarded as a masterpiece of Baroque art. A stone staircase leads up to portal which is flanked by two enormous columns set upon square bases. To the sides are niches holding the statues of Saint Giusto on the right and Saint Fortunato on the left. Above the balustrade with its alternating columns and pilasters is a statue of Saint Oronzo within an ornately decorated arch.

*Cathedral Square with the Cathedral, Bishop's
Palace and Seminary Palace*

Inside the Cathedral is built on a Latin cross design with three
naves. The beautiful coffered ceiling has paintings by Giuseppe
da Brindisi. The main altar is crafted with marble and gold-
plated bronze. There are twelve richly decorated side chapels
with paintings by Coppola, Domenico Catalano, Gianserio
Strafella, Giuseppe da Brindisi and Oronzo Tiso.

Torre Campanaria

The seventy-two metre high bell tower which stands to the left
of the Cathedral was added between 1661 and 1682 to replace
the Norman one which had crumbled in the seventeenth
century. It is divided into five tapered levels. The upper four
levels, each with a balustrade, have a single window on each
side while the highest has an octagonal majolica dome topped
with an iron statue of Saint Oronzo. If you climb to the top
there are wonderful views of the Adriatic Sea and also the
mountains of Albania on a clear day.

Palazzo Arcivescovile

The Bishop's Palace was first built in 1400, renovated in 1632 then completely restored in the eighteenth century by the architect Emanuele Manieri. The elegant façade is divided into three tiers with a series of rounded arches and balustrades. Above the main portal are three niches with statues, the central one being the Madonna. The upper level has a loggia with one of the oldest city clocks dating to 1761 in the gable. The building is topped with a two arched bell tower.

Seminario Palazzo

Building of the Seminary Palace began in 1694 and was completed in 1729. Taking up the entire western length of the square it is considered to be the finest Baroque architecture in Lecce. The mighty façade has two decorative lower levels divided by pilasters raised on pedestals and sixteen ornately framed windows. The central portal has a large balcony above it with three arched windows. The third level is more simplistic in design. It has nine windows and a stone balcony that runs the length of the building.

Inside there is an atrium, eight busts of the Doctors of the Church, a chapel and a beautiful cloister. The Museum of Sacred Art is housed in the building as well as a library containing over ten thousand books.

Walk north on the Piazza del Duomo then turn left onto Via Giuseppe Libertini. The Basilica di San Giovanni Battista del Rosario will be on the left after 350 metres.

Basilica di San Giovanni Battista del Rosario

The Basilica of Saint John the Baptist at the Rosary is one of the oldest churches in Lecce. It was designed by Giuseppe Zimbalo and built between 1691 and 1728. The stunning façade has a large portal over which rests a tympanum with the coats of arms of the Dominicans and a statue of San Domenico. Two huge spiral fluted columns stand on either side of the portal reaching up to the balustrade that divides the two levels. On each side of the columns are the statues of Saint John the Baptist and Saint Francis.

Above the balustrade, in the centre, is a statue of the Virgin as well as other niches holding statues, angels, horses and huge vases of flowers. At the top of the building stands the statue of Saint Thomas Aquinas.

Inside the church are thirteen altars surrounded by Baroque decorations. The coats of arms of families who contributed towards the church can be found at the bases of the pillars. There are numerous paintings and sculptures to view. Look out for the stone pulpit which is the only one to be found in Lecce.

The Main Façade of the Church of Saint John the Baptist

Walk west on Via Giuseppe Libertini for 50 metres and the Porta Rudiae will be ahead.

Porta Rudiae

The Rudiae Gate which takes its name from the destroyed city of Rudiae is the oldest and most stunning city gate in Lecce. It was built in 1703 by the nobleman Prospero Lubelli with a single rounded arch flanked by two columns on each side.

Above the arch is a statue of Saint Oronzo, the patron saint of Lecce. The gate is also known as Saint Oronzo gate. On either side are the statues of Saint Irene and Saint Dominic.

The Third Tour: Alberobello

Alberobello is a UNESCO World Heritage site and is regarded as the Capital of the Trulli. These are dry stone buildings with walls built without using mortar. The conical roofs use flat limestone slabs known as *chiancarelle*.

Alberobello's origins date back to the second half of the sixteenth century when the area was populated by forty peasant farmers who were granted land to farm there. They were ordered by the Counts of Conversano to build these dwellings without mortar. Built in this way the buildings could be quickly dismantled if there was a royal inspection so that taxes did not have to be paid to the Bourbons.

The citizens soon became discontent with demolishing their buildings before each inspection and on the 10th May 1707 seven courageous citizens met the Bourbon King Ferdinand requesting their independence from the Counts. The King agreed and sent a dispatch to Alberobello in which he sanctioned an end to the control of the feudal Counts of Conversano so that Alberobello at last became a free royal town.

Alberobello can be reached by car from places such as Brindisi airport or Bari within an hour. The scenic journey by train from Bari takes about an hour and a half and is very cheap. There are also trains from Taranto. Once in the town all the attractions are within walking distance. The train station in Alberobello is about a ten minute walk from the Piazza del Popolo in the centre of town. For a truly memorable experience stay overnight in one of the Trulli that have been converted to guest houses or hotels.

If you enjoy festivals then visit the town in spring or summer when there are festivals of jazz, classical, popular music, dance, street theatre and other things. The *Passion Festival* is held in Easter week. In July there is *the Re-enactment of the Expulsion of the Count of Conversano* while in August the *International Folk Festival* is held here as well as the *Festival del Sovrano* and *Beer within the Trulli* when you can listen to live concerts and taste different beers, local foods and other delicacies.

Today's tour begins at the tourist office located in Casa D'Amore in the Piazza Ferninando IV/ Piazza del Popolo. It takes you through the contrasting areas of Aia Piccola and Monti both of which have stunning views of the Trulli but while the first is a residential area the second is dominated by shops, restaurants, bars and cafes. It also offers the opportunity to visit museums, churches and to experience the magnificent views from different points around the town.

Main Sights
- Piazza Ferninando IV
- Casa d'Amore
- Piazza del Popolo
- Monumento ai Caduti
- Municipo di Alberobello
- Museo del Territorio "Casa Pezzolla"
- Rione Aia Piccola
- Museo dell'Olio
- Piazza Plebiscito
- Palazzo dei conti di Conversano
- Chiesa Santa Lucia/ Chiesa di San Giuseppe Artigiano
- Belvedere Santa Lucia
- Rione Monte
- Chiesa San Antonio di Padova
- Basilica dei Santa Mdici Cosma y Damiano
- Trullo Sovrano

Piazza Ferninando IV

This small square joins the Piazza del Popolo and has the main tourist office of Alberobello in the Casa d'Amore. Pick up a map of Alberobello here before crossing the Piazza del Popolo to start the tour.

Casa d'Amore

This building, which today houses the Alberobello tourist office, is named after its owner Francesco d'Amore who took part in the rebellion against the feudal tyranny in the eighteenth century. He was elected Mayor and when the dispatch came from the King that the people of Alberobello could build their homes using mortar if they wished he built this house in front of the Count of Conversano's Palace as a sign of victory.

Using lime and mortar which until that time had been forbidden materials the builders were able to construct a two-storey building which to them resembled a palace. A small balcony framed with an arch divides the façade. Look for the Latin inscription below the balcony stating that this house was the first in Alberobello to use lime. The Casa d'Amore was declared a national monument in 1930 due to its historical importance.

Piazza del Popolo

The People's Square is the main square in Alberobello and is surrounded by cafes, restaurants and places to sit. At night this area is full of life.

Monumento ai Caduti

The white marble obelisk that stands in the centre of the square is a memorial to the fallen of the Second World War, designed by the architect Antonio Curri Alberobellese. The names of

Alberobello's heroes are engraved on the bottom plinth. At each corner of the monument stands a small cannon with a helmet on top. Today it is regarded as a monument to those who have died in all the wars.

Municipo di Alberobello

The majestic Town Hall built in 1863 stands on the long side of the square. As well as housing government offices the police station is based here. The façade has symmetrical pilasters with balconies on the second floor and an impressive stone balustrade on the top. The lower floor has five portals.

Walk south on Piazza del Popolo then turn left onto Piazza XXVII Maggio. Cross over the roundabout and the Museo del Territorio "Casa Pezzolla" will be on the left.

Museo del Territorio "Casa Pezzolla"

The Territory Museum comprises a cluster of fifteen interconnecting Trulli that belonged to the doctor Giacomo Pezzolla. Today it is often referred to as *Casa Pezzola*, the House of Pezzola. In 1986 the group of Trulli was bought by the city of Alberobello and in the following years restored to its original state. As the only complex of this size it is protected by UNESCO.

There are two types of buildings making up this museum. The older ones which date back to the eighteenth century are mainly single interconnected cells built in the traditional dry stone way while the newer parts are spread over two floors with a high narrow façade and triangular pediment.

The museum has been furnished so that visitors can appreciate what life was like living in a Trulli in Alberobello at the end of the nineteenth century. It aims to raise awareness not only of the architectural features and material artefacts but of folk and cultural traditions too. As well as hosting temporary exhibitions the permanent exhibition holds displays of agricultural tools, building equipment and information about architectural traditions together with other artefacts and evidence that illustrate the Trulli customs.

The Trulli, with their conical roofs, were built from stones without using mortar like dry stone walls. This feature enabled more rooms to be added on easily as the family expanded. The walls were thick with few openings apart from the doorway to ensure any heat generated in winter was retained while the house remained cool in the hot summer.

Walk east on Piazza XXVII Maggio for 26 metres then continue onto Via Lamarmora for 75 metres. Turn right onto Via Galileo Galilei.

Rione Aia Piccola

Rione Aia Piccola is the oldest and most picturesque part of Alberobello, located in the south-eastern part of the town. It is a residential area and along its eight winding streets and alleys there are about four hundred Trulli. This is an area often neglected by tourists who are immediately drawn to the Rione Monti area that is full of Trulli converted to tourist shops.

As you wander around this authentic area of Aia Piccola you will enjoy a genuine atmosphere of calm. This was originally the agricultural area taking its name from *Aia*, a farmyard, used for the threshing of grain.

Trullli houses showing different roof symbols

The Trulli are all very similar but if you look carefully at the roofs as you wander through the area you will notice that the pinnacles at the top of the cone are different. These are often status symbols that showed either the skill of the builder or the wealth of the owners but may have been purely decoration. The symbols painted on the roofs such as a crescent, a pyramid, a star or a cross may be related to religion, occupation or even primitive or magical symbols.

Walk south on Via Galileo Galilei for 90 metres, turn left onto Via Giuseppe Verdi for 55 metres then take the first right onto Via Duca degli Abruzzi. Follow this road bearing right until you meet Via Guiseppe Verdi again and turn left. You will see the Museo dell'Olio after 6 metres.

Museo dell'Olio

The Oil Museum highlights the difference in the production of olive oil in the past to that today. It shows a short film about the different varieties of olives and the production of olive oil. There are displays with English translations of late nineteenth century tools including those used for milling and pressing olives as well as other exhibits of rural culture.

Walk north-west on Via Giuseppe Verdi for 40 metres then turn left onto via Brigata Regina. After 70 metres turn right onto Piazza Plebiscito.

Piazza Plebiscito

The Piazza Plebiscito is found at the southern end of the Piazza del Popolo and was where the people cast their votes. Where the two squares join there is a fountain built in 1996 that has a central column surrounded by four clay pots from which the water flows. From here you can see the Palace of the Counts, the Santa Lucia viewpoint and the Church of San Giuseppe Artigiano.

Palazzo dei Conti di Conversano

The Palace of the Counts of Conversano was constructed in 1635 by Count Gian Girolamo II. It was built not only as a hunting residence but also as a symbol of his importance in Alberobello. With thirteen rooms the building was suitable for court life with the upper floor divided into meeting rooms, a chapel and bedrooms.

The lower part of the building had basements that were used as a stable, a barn, a mill and a bakery as well as a blacksmith's workshop. The building still belongs to the heirs of the family.

> *Walk north-west on Piazza Plebiscito and turn left onto Piazza Giangirolamo. After 50 metres you will see Chiesa di San Giuseppe Artigiano and the Belvedere Santa Lucia.*

Chiesa Santa Lucia/ Chiesa di San Giuseppe Artigiano

The Church of Saint Lucia, also known as the Church of Joseph the Worker, was first built in the early nineteenth century to house the Brotherhood of the Blessed Sacrament but restored and enlarged in the second half of the nineteenth century. It was then dedicated to Santa Lucia, the protector of Alberobello. A relic of Santa Lucia was obtained from Venice in 1904 on the authorisation of Bishop Antonio Lamberti to place within the church.

It is a small Baroque church with a sombre façade, the only decoration being a mixed-line window in the centre above the entrance door. Behind this stands a square bell tower topped with a pointed dome which mimics the shape of the Trulli. Four short square pillars topped with pinnacles stand at each corner.

Inside the church is a single nave with a presbytery. A large window is all that lights the entire church. The nineteenth century carving of Christ is by an unknown artist. Look out for the statue of Saint Francis of Assisi and the two statues of Madonna. Just beyond the church is the Belvedere Santa Lucia.

View of Trulli Houses from Belvedere Santa Lucia

Belvedere Santa Lucia

The Saint Lucia viewpoint is a wonderful place to stand and admire the impressive sight of the tiny streets climbing up the hill lined with the Trulli of Rione Monti. This is a great place to take photographs.

Walk south then take the stairs down and turn right onto Largo Martellotta. After 35 metres turn left onto Via Monte San Michele.

Rione Monte

Rione Monte, which translates as the *Mountain District,* is located to the south-west of Alberobello. It is the main tourist part of Alberobello filled with tourist shops, bars, restaurants and cafes yet it has still managed to retain its charm. Several narrow lanes slope up the hill while others wind across lined with around one thousand Trulli. It is very picturesque and there are some stunning views.

Many vendors will try to entice you inside the shops and bars with their wares or panoramic terraces that offer fantastic views. It is worth entering for the experience of being inside a Trulli. The bars provide the opportunity to sample local wines while there will be many opportunities to purchase the local terracotta whistles, ceramics, jewellery, biscuits, pasta and other souvenirs.

Walk for 200 metres along Via Monte San Michele. Continue onto Piazza Gabriele D'Annunzio for 20 metres then onto Via Monte Pertica. The Chiesa San Antonio di Padova will be on the left after 110 metres.

Chiesa San Antonio di Padova

The Church of Saint Antony of Padova was built in fourteen months and opened in 1927. It stands at the top of the Rione Monti hill and is a fascinating church build to mimic the Trulli so characteristic of Alberobello.

It is built on a Greek cross design with side chapels. The church has Apulian-Romanesque architectural elements such as the beautiful rose window that dominates the façade. The central dome that is around twenty metres tall has a skylight surrounded by four small cupolas crowned with pinnacles.

Although the entrance is grand the interior of the church is quite sober and simplistic with the only colour being the twentieth century fresco covering the altar wall. This is by the artist Aldolfo Rollo and depicts the *Tree of Life*.

The church of Saint Antony of Padova

Walk east on Via Monte Pertica for 120 metres then turn left onto Via Monte Sabotino, left after 200 metres onto Largo Martellotta then left again after 20 metres onto Via Balenzano. After 90 metres continue onto Via Umberto for 20 metres, Vico Tenente Cuccdi for 90 metres, Corso Vittorio Emanuele for 150 metres and Piazza Curri for 55 metres. Turn right onto Via Monte Calvario. The Basilica of Saints Cosma and Damiano will be on the left after 20 metres.

Basilica dei Santa Medici Cosma y Damiano

In 1635 the Count of Conversano built a small church in Alberobello to show his devotion to the *Santa Medici*, the patron saints of doctors. A painting of the Madonna between Saint Cosmos and Saint Damian was placed upon the altar. Little by little this church was enlarged and then in 1880's the present basilica, designed by the local architect Antonio Curri was constructed.

The Church of the Patron Saint of Doctors

The majestic Neo-Classical façade has long pilasters and fluted columns with Corinthian capitals. It has two spectacular bell towers that stand thirty-six metres high, each topped with a pointed steeple. A stone balcony runs between them and underneath each is a clock.

The ornate portal is decorated by the four moral virtues and medallions that symbolise the theological virtues. In the porch above the door are engravings of Jesus being crucified between Mary, Saint John, Saint Peter, Saint Paul, Saint Cosmos and Saint Damian.

Inside the church is richly decorated with Gospel scenes and fine frescos. There are some interesting wood carvings and also internal vaults. Behind the church there are two small lanes of Trulli leading to the Trullo Sovrano.

Continue north on Via Monte Calvario for 40 metres, turn left onto Via Santi Cosma e Damiano for 50 metres, right onto Via del Gesù for 35 metres, right again onto Vico Ten O Gigante and the Trullo Sovrano will be on the left after 10 metres.

Trullo Sovrano

The building known as the Trullo Sovrano or *Trullo of the King*, is Alberobello's largest Trullo building and the only example in the modern part of the town of a Trullo with two floors. It was declared a National Monument in 1930. Originally built in the mid-eighteenth century by the Cataldo Peerta family today it is a small privately owned museum that offers an insight into Trulli life.

This Trullo is on a grand scale and furnished authentically. Inside there is a bakery, bedroom and kitchen and a souvenir shop that stocks a wealth of information about the town as well as items such as traditional Alberobello recipe books. There are information boards with English translations. Look out for the spy-hole next to the door that allowed the residents to vet their visitors.

If you want to extend this tour you could visit the Wine Museum in Via Due Macelli which is about 800 metres away or return to the main street of Largo Martellotta and Piazza del Popolo where the tour began.

To return to Piazza del Popolo walk south-west on Vico Ten O Gigante for 10 metres, turn left onto Via Gesù for 85 metres then left onto Piazza Antonio Curri for 100 metres until you meet Corso Vittorio Emanuele. After 220 metres turn left onto Piazza del Popolo.

The Fourth Tour: Matera

Matera, famous for its cave-dwellings known as the *Sassi,* was named a UNESCO World Heritage Site in 1993 and selected as the European Capital of Culture for 2019. Situated in the remote southern region of Basilica the city is still little visited but travellers to this historic centre will be transported back in time and amazed by the breathtaking views. The area has been inhabited since Palaeolithic times. Walking through the narrow streets and alleyways, entering the caves or rock churches and enjoying the landscape from the viewpoints will provide experiences never to be forgotten.

A small street in the Sassi

The area around Matera is often regarded as the *Second Bethlehem*. Wander through the Sassi and you will understand why Mel Gibson chose to film the *Passion of Christ* here. Matera is hilly and there are many steps so the walking tours should not be attempted if you have any problem with mobility. However, you could still visit the newer part of the town and enjoy the Sassi from viewpoints such as Belvedere Piazzetta Pascoli.

Matera is about forty miles from Bari and its airport. There is a free bus known as the *Pugliair* bus that runs a few times a day in the summer months but it is also possible to take the train from Bari to Matera. The scenic train journey is very cheap and takes around an hour and a half. Take care to plan your trip carefully as at present there are no services on Sundays or public holidays. There are also buses from Taranto.

In order to explore Matera properly you need to spend at least two days here. Read through this guide and decide which museums or churches you really want to visit then choose your days. Some attractions are only open at weekends, especially during the winter months. They may need to be booked so do your research online to find opening times and other relevant information. Matera has a number of hotels and Guest Houses. For a real unique experience why not stay in one of the converted caves.

The first tour of Matera starts and ends in the Piazza Vittorio Veneto with its elegant palaces and churches. It explores the oldest part of the city known as the Civita that stood on the plateau within the city walls until the sixteenth century and looked over the ravine known locally as the *Gravina*.

As well as visiting the Cathedral, beautiful palaces, churches and museums you will see parts of the old city wall and its towers. Try to fit in a visit to Casa Noha that will explain why people came to live in the rocks and then abandoned them.

Tomorrow's tour ends at the Piazza Duomo so if you are short of time today you could visit today's last four attractions after completing tomorrow's tour instead.

Main Sights:

- Piazza Vittorio Veneto
- Palazzo del Governo
- Palazzo dell'Annunziata
- Chiesa San Domenico
- Chiesa Santo Spirito
- Palombaro Lungo
- Belvedere Luigi Guerricchio
- Fontana Ferdinandea
- Chiesa San Francesco d'Assisi
- Piazza and Palazzo del Sedile
- Museo della Fotografia Pino Settanni
- Casa Noha
- Palazzo Visconte
- Piazza Duomo
- Palazzo Malvinni Malvezzi
- Cattedrale di Matera
- Torre Metellana
- Chiesa di Sant'Agostino
- Museo della Tortura
- Chiesa di San Giovanni Battista

Piazza Vittorio Veneto

Piazza Vittorio Veneto is Matera's beautiful central square that was established in 1880. The square is surrounded by elegant palaces and churches built by the wealthy to cover up the poverty of those who lived in the Sassi. Make sure you visit the Tourist Office situated here where you can pick up a map and other information about the city.

Pulsating with life the square has a number of attractions, some of which are below street level and easy to miss. The ancient Sassi together with the underground part of Matera can be accessed from here. Walk down the steps to the Barisano stone area and see parts of the old city that was discovered during development work in the 1990's.

If you are staying for a few days in Matera then you will have time to return to the square in order to spend a few hours looking at the attractions in detail. There are also a number of places where you can take refreshments and enjoy the atmosphere.

Palazzo del Governo

The Governor's Palace stands at the north-western corner of Piazza Vittorio Veneto next to the Church of San Domenico. With its yellow coloured façade, steel balconies and beautiful decorated door it is a striking building.

Palazzo dell'Annunziata

The majestic eighteenth century Palace of the Annunciation can be found dominating the western side of the Piazza. Built in 1735 it originally belonged to the Dominican Sisters of Santa Maria la Nova but today is home to the provincial library, a media library and a cinema.

The Palace of the Annunciation

The façade is divided into two levels with cornices and arches. The central arch was meant to give access to a church built in the mid-nineteenth century that was never consecrated. A roof garden and café on the top provide a breath-taking view. In front of the building there is a large circular fountain.

Chiesa San Domenico

The Church of Saint Domenico was founded in 1230 and was part of a complex that included a convent. The Italian poet Giovani Pascoli lived here for two years while he was teaching in Matera. The façade of the church is Romanesque in style although the original gabled roof has been replaced during the seventeenth century with a tuff barrel vault.

A *telemone* supports the beautiful rose window representing the *Wheel of Life* while a carving of a deacon embellishes each side. Above the window a carving shows the Archangel Michael defeating the dragon. A dog carrying a torch in its mouth, a symbol of the Dominicans representing the Lord's guard dog, can be seen in the centre of the window.

Inside the church there are three naves and a transept that have been modified during the eighteenth century and decorated with stucco. On entry the tomb of Orazio Persio can be seen on the right. There are a number of interesting paintings and statues. The octagonal *Chapel of the Rosary* is worth viewing as well as the small majolica font.

Chiesa Santo Spirito

The small rectangular Church of the Holy Spirit is a Rupestrian church built around the end of the eighth century and is accessed through a gate and down the steps from the Piazza Vittorio Veneto.

The façade is plain but has small bell towers while the roof is pitched with a layer of tiles. Inside a few frescos can still be seen although they are in a poor condition. One shows Saint Sophia protected by shields while at the bottom of the nave there are traces of another portraying Christ.

Palombaro Lungo

The *Long Diver* is also accessed by the steps leading down from the Piazza Vittorio Veneto. Built in the nineteenth century it is the largest water storage tank in Matera and is situated right under the square. It was built to store water for the surrounding buildings using not only rainwater but also a natural source located on the Tramontano Castle hill. As the population increased in size many modifications were made to increase its capacity.

Belvedere Luigi Guerricchio

The Luigi Guerricchio viewpoint located in Piazza Vittorio Veneto provides one of the best views of the old city. From here it is possible to pick out the locations where scenes from Mel Gibson's *Passion of Christ* were filmed.

Fontana Ferdinandea

The Ferdinando Fountain can be found at the southern end of Piazza Vittorio Veneto. Having been located at the foot of Castle Hill to collect water it was restored and erected on the foundations of another fountain by King Ferdinand II in 1832.

After World War II the fountain was moved to the town park but in 2009 returned to its original location in Piazza Vittorio Veneto. The emblem of the city, a royal crown and cross, can be seen on the upper part of the fountain while in the rectangular area below is an inscription written in Latin describing its rebuilding by King Ferdinand.

From the Fontana Ferdinandea walk southeast for 23 metres and continue onto Via del Corso. After 160 metres turn left onto Piazza San Francesco then right after 10 metres. The Church of Saint Francis of Assisi will be on the left after 55 metres.

Piazza and Chiesa San Francesco D'Assisi

The Church of Saint Francis of Assisi is located at the entrance of Piazza San Francesco. The building dates back to the thirteenth century but has been modified a number of times over the years. In 1670 it was almost completely rebuilt in Baroque style with its two storey façade divided by a corniced string course. The portal and five windows are decorated with delicate plant scrolls while a statue of the Virgin Mary stands within a central niche on the upper floor embellished with angels holding luxurious baroque stone drapes. The statue of Saint Francis can be seen on the left while on the right is the statue of Saint Anthony of Padua.

Chiesa San Francesco d'Assisi

Inside the church has a single nave with side chapels and a finely sculptured stone font by the entrance door. In the first chapel there is a statue of Saint Anthony by the sculptor Stefano da Putignano and the sarcophagus of Eustachio Paulicelli who is locally known as the *Lawyer of the Poor*. The *Immaculate Conception* by Antonio Stabile can be seen in the second chapel.

In the third chapel there is a trapdoor leading to the ancient crypt of Saint Peter and Saint Paul. Here you can see some of Matera's oldest frescos. The fifteenth century altarpiece which was the work of Lazzaro Bastiani is divided into nine panels and regarded as the most important item held in the church.

From the Church of Saint Francis of Assisi walk south-east for 30 metres then turn left onto Via San Francesco D'Assisi. After 40 metres turn left onto Piazza del Sedile.

Piazza Sedile

The Piazza Sedile, which translates as *the Square of the Seat* was originally known as Piazza Maggiore, *the Greater Square*. In the fourteenth century it was a merchants' square surrounded by warehouses as well as shops and inns. In the sixteenth century the house of the city governor with the town hall or *Seat of Government* together with the city jails were situated here. Today it is a good place to visit in order to enjoy these beautiful buildings or to relax and take refreshment.

Palazzo del Sedile

The Palace of the Seat is the most important building in the Piazza Sedile. It was built by the Archbishop Saraceno in 1540 as a seat for the town meetings. Restored in 1779 it has since been modified. Today it is home to the Conservatory of Music.

A large arched entrance bordered by two bell towers can be seen on the façade. One bell tower has a clock while the other has a sundial. The façade is also decorated with six statues. The two above the centre represent the patron saints guarding the city; Sant'Eustachio on the left and the Madonna della Bruna on the right. The four cardinal virtues of justice, fortitude, temperance and prudence that provide an allegory for good government can be seen in the niches.

Walk to the northern end of the Piazza del Sedile then turn right onto Via Duomo. Continue for 180 metres until you reach Piazza Duomo turning right onto Via San Potito. You will pass the Museum of Photography, Casa Noha and several old palaces that have now become hotels. Continue until Palazzo Viceconte which is now a hotel.

Museo della Fotografia Pino Settanni

The Pino Settanni Photography museum opened in 2015 five years after the death of Pino Settanni. The City of Matera sponsored it and dedicated the museum to the man who took so many photographs of this area so that all his works could be housed in one place.

Casa Noha

The Noha House is a traditional old building built into the tuff rock. The twelve rooms have been renovated to become a tourist information centre with a multimedia exhibition showing a movie of the *Invisible Sassi* that takes the visitor on a journey through Matera and the Sassi explaining why people came to live in the rocks and then abandoned them.

Palazzo Visconte

The Palace of the Viscount of Matera has been renovated and turned into an hotel. Situated in this historic part of the city it has magnificent views over the Sassi if you climb to the terrace on the top floor.

It is possible to go inside to see the attractive eighteenth century court and the monumental staircase that leads to the main rooms. At the top there are antiques and paintings that range from the seventeenth to twentieth centuries.

Walk back along Via San Potito until you reach Piazza Duomo where you can visit the Cathedral and other buildings. Note that the next tour ends in the Piazza Duomo so you could visit the Cathedral and other attractions tomorrow if you prefer.

Piazza Duomo

Cathedral Square offers a wonderful vista over the Sassi and surrounding area. In the sixteenth century many of the nobles had their homes around this part of the city so there are a number of interesting buildings nearby to view, including the Cathedral itself.

Palazzo Malvinni Malvezzi

The Malvinni Malvezzi Palace overlooks Cathedral Square and was built in the sixteenth century. It belonged to the Malvinni Malvezzi family who originally came from Bologna in the fifteenth century and held the title of the Santa Candida Duchy. The building is divided into three levels and has eighteenth century majolica tiled paving. There are fourteen exquisite paintings on the ground floor and other interesting items such as chandeliers, mirrors and Louis XVI style furniture to view.

Matera Cathedral

The building is also known as the *Kittens Palace*. Count Francesco Kittens trying to escape from the uprising in the city came to a sticky end when he jumped from the palace fracturing his legs. Although he initially escaped he was captured later the same day and killed with a dagger.

Cattedrale di Matera

The Romanesque Cathedral of Matera was built in the thirteenth century on the Civita old town ridge that divides the two regions of the Sassi. It is located at the highest point and dominates the city.

There is a statue of the *Madonna della Bruna*, the city's patron saint, bordered with intricate carving over the main door with statues of Saint Peter and Saint Paul in the niches on each side. In the centre the rose window has sixteen rays representing the *Wheel of Fortune* while above is the Archangel Michael overpowering the dragon. There are four small columns representing Mathew, Mark, Luke and John as well as twelve half columns thought to represent the apostles.

The building has two monumental doors on the side façade. The Porta di Piazza has a carving of Abraham the father of Christianity, Judaism and Islam as a message for the three religious communities that lived in Matera at the time. The Porta dei Leoni door has two statues of lions symbolising the guardians of the faith. Between the doors is a delicately engraved glass window. The fifty-two metre tall bell tower is divided by a balcony with mullioned windows. The spire is crowned with an orb and cross.

The Cathedral is built on the Latin cross design and has three naves. Inside there is a Byzantine fresco of the *Madonna della Bruna and Child* and a fourteenth century fresco portraying *the Last Judgment*. The high altar that came from the Abbey of Montescaglioso has been constructed from white marble. The intricate sculptured wooden choir behind the altar is the work of Giovanni Tantino of Ariano Irpin.

Look out for the crib in the Chapel of San Nicola al Cimitero that contains features of the city of Matera such as the castle at the top that resembles Castello Tramontano.

Walk south across the Piazza then turn right onto Via Gradoni Duomo. After 20 metres bear right to stay on this road for another 150 metres before making a slight right onto Via San Nicola del Sole. After 40 metres you will see Torre Metellana.

Torre Metellana

The Metellana tower was originally part of the defensive city walls that together with the River Gravina ravine made the city almost impenetrable. There were once six towers situated along the city walls paid for by the brave Captain Metello who won many victories over the Saracens before making Matera his home. The tower was named after him.

Walk south-east on Via San Nicola del Sole for 40 metres then turn right onto Gradelle San Nicola del Sole. After 80 metres bear right onto Via D'Addozio. The Convent of Saint Agostino will be on the right after 280 metres.

Chiesa di Sant'Agostino

The Church of Saint Augustine was formerly a monastery and has been painstakingly restored. The monastery was created in 1592 by monks from the Order of Hermits over an underground chamber built by the Augustinians in the eleventh century and dedicated to Saint William. For a small fee it is possible to visit the crypt of this Rupestrian rock church which can be accessed from the left hand side of the main altar to view the ancient frescos.

The façade of the main church, known also as Santa Maria delle Grazie, is of Baroque style and divided into two levels. The lower level has a portal with a carved wooden door surrounded by a niche with a statue of Saint Augustine. Above the window on the second level there is another niche with a statue of a bishop blessing Saint Peter and Saint Paul who stand to each side of the pillars. The square bell tower can be seen between the church and the monastery.

The church was built in 1595 on the Latin cross design comprising a single nave with side altars that are divided by pillars and half columns topped with capitals decorated with acanthus leaves. The interior is richly decorated with carvings and paintings by artists from Naples as well as local craftsmen.

Chiesa di Sant'Agostino

The wooden pulpit between the second and third altars dates from the eighteenth century and has a baldachin with a central medallion while the organ has gilded and painted pipes dating from 1770. To the right of the main altar in the transept, surmounted by a dome, is the statue of Saint Augustine while on the left is the statue of Saint Vito.

Look out for the baptismal font that uses stone from San Pietro Barisano and the Augustinian coat of arms that depicts the heart of Jesus pierced by an arrow standing on a book.

Walk north-west on Via D'Addozio for 80 metres then turn left to stay on this road. Bear right after 5 metres, continue for 65 metres then turn left onto Via Santo Stefano. After 15 metres turn right onto Via Gian Battista Pentasugli. The Museo della Tortura is 8 metres along this road on the left.

Museo della Tortura

The Museum of Torture holds a collection of around one hundred original instruments of torture from the sixteenth and seventeenth centuries that demonstrate what people were willing to do to others in the name of religion.

Walk east on Via Gian Battista Penasuglia for 8 metres. Turn right onto Via Santo Stefano, continue onto Via Santa Casarea for 220 metres, onto Via San Biagio for 100 metres then onto Piazza Giavani. The Chiesa di San Giovanni Battista will be on the right.

Chiesa di San Giovanni Battista

The Romanesque Saint John the Baptist church was built in 1233 and was originally known as Santa Maria la Nova. Today it is one of the most important preserved examples of medieval architecture in southern Italy.

The original portal has been superimposed by an eighteenth century arch in order to strengthen it but it is still possible to see the intricate and elaborate decorations of the original by Michele Del Giudice and Marco Di Lauria. Above the portal is a niche with an eighteenth century stone statue of Saint John the Baptist and a small rose window.

Like many other churches it is built on the Latin cross design and has three naves that are divided by large pillars with quatrefoils and other elaborate decorations. The architecture is typically medieval. Look out for the fresco of *Santa Maria la Nova* and also for the exquisite wooden carvings.

Walk south-west on Via San Biagio for 130 metres then continue for 50 metres onto Piazza Vittorio Veneto where this circular tour started.

The Fifth Tour: More Matera

Not many years ago Matera's Sassi was known as the *Shame of Italy* for its dismal poverty and slum like dwellings that were blighted with Malaria. The living conditions of these people who were mainly peasants and farmers were dreadful. It was not until the 1950's that the entire population of around sixteen thousand people was moved from the Sassi and relocated in the modern city.

Although some people resisted the move and remained in the Sassi it was basically just an empty shell. Today people with enough money have moved back into the area turning it into upmarket homes, guest houses and hotels. Those who have returned can claim they are living in the same houses as their ancestors who lived here nine thousand years ago.

Today's tour begins at the Piazza San Francesco and ends at the Piazza Duomo; both places visited yesterday. There will be opportunities to see Matera and the Sassi from different viewpoints and compare different districts. As well as visiting rock churches, palaces and museums you will go down into the Sassi district and have the chance to visit a refurbished cave home and the graves in the Barbaric Cemetery.

If you have a map you will notice that there are a number of occasions on the tour when you are near things listed yesterday. If you didn't have time to see everything you could make a slight detour to see anything you missed.

Main Attractions

- Chiesa del Purgatorio
- Chiesa Santa Chiara
- Museo Archeologico Nazionale "Domenico Ridola"
- Piazzetta Giovanni Pascoli
- Palazzo Lanfranchi
- Belvedere Piazzetta Pascoli
- Santa Lucia alle Malve
- Cimitero Barbarico
- Casa Grotta di Vico Solitario
- Chiesa di San Pietro e Paolo Caveoso
- MUSMA – Museo della Scultura Contemporanea
- Porta Pistola

Detail on door of Chiesa del Purgatorio

Walk south-east on Piazza San Francesco, turn right onto Via San Francesco D'Assisi for 60 metres then left onto Via Domenico Ridola. The Chiesa del Purgatorio will be on the right after 35 metres.

Chiesa del Purgatorio

The Purgatory Church was completed in 1747 using funds from the Brotherhood of the Poor and donations from Matera citizens who also helped to build it. It is only a small church but well worth a visit for its frescos, decorations and works of art.

Giuseppe Fatone was responsible for the Baroque façade that is decorated along the theme of death and the redemption of souls. The curved façade is divided into two parts with a carving of the Madonna and Child in the upper niche, decorations of angels, garlands of flowers and flames enveloping repentant souls. On the lower level a carving of the Archangel Michael stands in the right niche while the Archangel Raphael stands in the left.

The wooden portal is divided into thirty-six panels each decorated on the death theme with skulls and crossbones of priests, royalty and ordinary citizens in order to demonstrate the equality of everyone in death.

Inside the church has an octagonal dome supported by Corinthian capitals. In the eight sections Saint Matthew, Saint Mark, Saint Luke, Saint John, Saint Ambrose, Saint Gerome Saint Augustine and Saint Gregory are depicted. There are three altars with paintings of the *Death of Saint Joseph, San Gaetano interceding with the Virgin Mary* and *Saint Nicholas of Tolentino and the Virgin.*

Other paintings include the *Kiss of Judas* and the *Crucifixion* as well as superb scenes from *the Passion* and pictures of *San Francesco Paolo, Saint Anthony of Padua* and the *Madonna of the Rosary* to whom the organ dated from 1755 is dedicated.

From the Chiesa del Purgatorio walk south-east on Via Domenico Ridola for 45 metres. The Chiesa Santa Chiara will be on the right. You will also see the Matera Congress building on the left.

Chiesa Santa Chiara

The Church of Saint Chiara was built in the late seventeenth century as part of a group of buildings for the training college for priests. The façade is richly decorated and has a lunette on the upper part with a niche above that represents God's blessing. In the central niche below is a statue of Madonna del Carmine.

In the lower level a statue of Santa Chiara stands on the right and a statue of San Francisco on the left. Between the statues is an eighteenth century wooden door surrounded by decorations and enclosed by two pillars. The coat of arms of Bishop Ryos can be seen above.

The church has a nave with a barrel vault and arched lancet. There are beautiful wooden altars along the side walls. Two plates depicting Saint Agnes and Saint Rose of Lima can be seen on the main altar while on the high altar is a painting of the *Madonna of the Angels*. Look out for the stunning wooden pulpit, the statue of Saint Clare kneeling in prayer and other paintings such as the *Presentation of Mary in the temple*.

The Church of Saint Chiara

Continue along Via Domenico Ridola for 18 metres. The Museo Archeologico Nazionale "Domenico Ridola" will be on the right.

Museo Archeologico Nazionale "Domenico Ridola"

The National Archaeological Museum of Ridola Matera established in 1911 is the oldest museum in the region. It is housed in the old convent of Santa Chiara. The senator and doctor Ridola left a will donating his archaeological collections to the town. Today it holds collections from prehistoric times until the Middle Ages.

Continue walking south-east on Via Domenico Ridola for 30 metres. Make a slight left to stay on this road for another 70 metres before turning left onto Piazzetta Pascoli.

Piazzetta Giovanni Pascoli

The Giovanni Pascoli Square is named after the Italian poet Giovanni Pascoli who lived in Matera between 1882 and 1884 when he taught Latin and Greek in the schools. The Palazzo Lanfranchi is situated on this square and next to it is the point from which you can enjoy one of the most spectacular views of the Sassi.

Palazzo Lanfranchi

The Lanfranchi Palace is today the home of the National Museum of Medieval and Modern Art. The Palace was built by Friar Francesco da Copertino in the seventeenth century. The beautiful building has an asymmetric façade divided into two horizontal levels by a cornice.

The upper level has ten columns forming nine blind arches, one of which has a rose window. The lower level has five niches that hold the statues of saints such as Madonna del Carmine while the top of the building is crowned with a pediment with a clock inside.

The National Museum of Medieval and Modern Art is divided into four areas: Sacred Arts, Contemporary Arts, the Demo Ethno Anthropological section and the Collecting area.

From the museum walk back north-west along Via Domenico Ridola and take the stairs. After 25 metres turn right onto Piazzetta Pascoli where there is a magnificent view of the Sassi.

Belvedere Piazzetta Pascoli

The Pascoli viewpoint has stunning views of the two Sassi districts and the landscape you see from the balcony will never be forgotten. The *Civita* or old town and the Sasso Caveoso can be admired from this point. The Via Bruno Buozzi, the old Sassi road that winds down into Sasso Caveoso can be accessed from the square.

View of the Civita and Sassi from Belvedere Piazzetta Pascoli

Walk south-east on Calata Domenico Ridola for 38 metres. Turn left to stay on this road. After 25 metres turn right onto Vico Mannesi, continue for 65 metres, turn left onto Vico Confalone then right after 16 metres onto Via Purgatorio Vecchio for 20 metres.

Turn left onto Via Bruno Buozzi then right after 10 metres onto Via Rione Malve. Staying on Via Rione Malve turn right after 15 metres, right after 10 metres, left after 20 metres and a slight left after 8 metres. Chiesa Santa Lucia alle Malve will be ahead.

Santa Lucia alle Malve

The Church of Saint Lucy of the Mallows is a rock church that dates from the eighth century and was the first female monastic settlement in Matera. The monastery has a number of entrances along the rock wall but the entrance to the church is on the right bordered by square tufa blocks and a pointed arch and lunette with a symbol of the saint inside.

Inside the church there are ancient frescos that have survived well due to the technique used by the Matera fresco painters of the time even though some are over one thousand years' old. After conservation work these works of historic and artistic importance have been returned to their original splendour.

Look out for the frescos of *Madonna del Latte,* the *Coronation of the Virgin,* the picture of *Saint Vito* considered to be the patron saint against Saint Vitus Dance and the statue of *Saint Michael the Archangel.*

Walk south on Rione Malve for 3 metres, turn left onto Vico Solitario, right after 55 metres to stay on this road then right again after 12 metres. Continue along Vico Solitario for 55 metres where you will find the Cimitero Barbarico.

Cimitero Barbarico

The graves of the Barbaric Cemetery are carved into the bedrock. They appear much smaller than our graves today but the people of the time were much shorter than us. Look carefully and you will see the part of the grave where the tombstone could be joined. Today many of the graves have been covered with cement and pebbles in order to preserve them while maintaining their original shape.

Bronze remains have also been found on this site. They include the holes where the supporting posts for huts were inserted as well as skeletal remains.

Walk north on Vico Solitario for 65 metres. The Casa Grotta di Vico Solitario will be on the left.

Casa Grotta di Vico Solitario

The cave-house in the Vico Solitario neighbourhood is now a museum furnished with authentic furniture and tools to enable visitors to understand what life was like for people living in the Sassi before being forced to leave and rehoused due to the terrible conditions. The Sassi had become a symbol of national shame.

There is a picture of the family who lived in this cave-house until 1957 with no drinking water or toilets. The home is accessed through a hole in the rock. It is possible to see the kitchen in the centre with a fireplace and a small table. On the table is a single dish from which the family ate their frugal meals. Nearby is the bed raised above the floor so that there was no contact with the animals that lived in the stable at the end of the cave.

Walk back north onto Vico Solitario and continue for 70 metres onto Piazza San Pietro Caveoso. The Chiesa di San Pietro Caveoso will be on the left after 5 metres.

Chiesa di San Pietro e Paolo Caveoso

The spectacular Church of Saint Peter and Paul is the only church in the Sassi not dug into the tufa rock. It dates from 1218 although the building has undergone many changes and renovations over the years so that many original features have disappeared.

In the seventeenth century the whole church was completely renovated with the interior being enlarged and side chapels added together with a new Baroque style façade and bell tower. The bell tower is divided into three levels with a balcony and balustrade carved with geometric patterns. The top culminates in a pyramid-shaped tower.

The façade has three portals with a number of niches housing statues. On the left is Saint Peter and on the right Saint Paul, both with rectangular windows above. In the centre is Our Lady of Mercy with two mullioned windows and a circular window above.

Chiesa di San Pietro e Paolo Caveoso

At the end of the nave is an eighteenth century altar with a wooden altarpiece portraying the *Madonna and Child with Saint Peter and Saint Paul* and a picture of the *Last Supper*. There were originally eight chapels off the central nave but those on the right have been removed to create an oratory and archway. In the chapels there are paintings, frescos and wooden altarpieces.

Walk north-west on Piazza San Pietro Caveoso onto Via Bruno Buozzi for 45 metres. Turn right to stay on this road for 30 metres, make a slight left onto Via Rione Pianelle for 45 metres, bearing left again to stay on Via Rione Pianelle for 45 metres.

Make a sharp right onto Via Muro. Continue for 40 metres, bear right onto Via San Giacomo, then left after 50 metres to stay on this road. After 65 metres the Museo della Scultura Contemporanea will be on the left.

MUSMA – Museo della Scultura Contemporanea

The Musma Museum of Contemporary Sculpture is the most important museum in Italy dedicated to sculpture. It is located in the seventeenth century Palazzo Pomarici, often known as the *Palace of Hundred Rooms.*

The museum holds about four hundred items including sculptures, ceramics, jewellery, medals, drawings and prints that are located not only in the built up part of the palace but also in the seven caves carved from tuff below. The library has over five thousand books and offers a place to study and research.

Walk south-west on Via San Giacomo for 27 metres. Turn left onto Via Sant'Angelo. After 66 metres bear left for 8 metres then right onto Via Ospedale Vecchio for 50 metres and left onto Via Madonna delle Virtù for 20 metres. Turn right and you will reach Porta Pistola after 50 metres.

Porta Pistola

The Porta Pistola, which translates as *the Door of the Gun* is a car park and viewing point over the spectacular landscape of the Sassi and the Gravina below. There is a pizzeria here where you can take refreshment and enjoy the view.

Walk north on Via Madonna delle Virtù for 46 metres. Turn left onto Recinto II Ospedale Vecchio. After 35 metres turn right onto Via San Potito and continue for 190 metres onto Piazza Duomo.

Final Thoughts

These tours were written in response to guided tours that the author attended whilst in Puglia, all of which tended to rush the participants from one location to the next and only included the most popular tourist sights. The walks in this book have been designed to introduce you to the charms of Puglia while exploring four very different towns and cities. They will take you to a range of attractions so that you can get a balanced view of each location.

You will appreciate why Brindisi has been known as the *Gateway to the East* since its development as a port for the Roman troops and later for the merchants of Venice by visiting its Roman Columns at the end of the Appian Way and city gates. Hopefully you will have seen the Saint Pietro of Schiavoni Archeological Area where the sympathetic construction of the modern theatre has enabled the mediaeval and Roman dwellings to be preserved and viewed.

In Lecce you will have seen evidence of the Roman occupation of the city by visiting the amphitheatre and Roman theatre and also understand why the town is known as the *Florence of the South* having visited the numerous Baroque buildings and churches built in the seventeenth century.

When visiting such contrasting locations as Alberobello and Matera you will acknowledge the importance of making these places UNESCO World Heritage sites. You will marvel at the unique construction of the Trulli houses in Alberobello and be astounded that people still lived in the Sassi slums of Matera as late as the 1950's

There may not be time to explore the interior of every building or visit all museums included in each day's walking tour so a section for your own notes is included over the next few pages. Here you may wish to make notes of places to visit if you have any spare time on another day, or intend to return to Puglia in the future. You may also wish to write down things such as restaurants where you have enjoyed the traditional Apulian food or favourite attractions that you can pass onto friends.

NOTES

NOTES

NOTES

NOTES

NOTES

You may also enjoy reading...

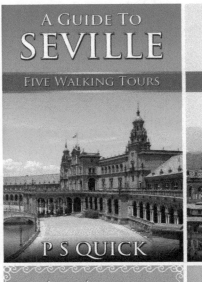